MW00658606

Ms. Frances Fulkerson
1302 White Oak Trl
Godfrey, IL 62035

TREATMENT

TREATMENT

How Prayer in Christian Science Transforms Consciousness and Heals

William D. Kilpatrick

The Bookmark
Santa Clarita, California

Kilpatrick, William Duncan.
Treatment: how prayer in Christian Science transforms consciousness and heals / William Duncan Kilpatrick. -1st ed.
p. cm.
LCCN 2001098223
ISBN 0-930227-41-7

1. Christian Science. 2. Prayer. 3. Spiritual healing. 4. Metaphysics. I. Title.
BX6943.K55 2002 289.5
QBI33-279

Published by
The Bookmark
Post Office Box 801143
Santa Clarita, California 91380

INTRODUCTION

In recent years students of Christian Science have been returning to the early days of the movement when profound works on Christian Science were being written. Many of these papers were by Christian Science teachers who wrote them as an association address for students who had had class instruction with them.

These teachers had a deep understanding of God, evidenced by their healing works, and they poured into their addresses their most inspired thoughts. Mr. Kilpatrick was counted among the finest of these early teachers. Throughout his writings he emphasizes how our lives are determined by our thoughts. He then explains how the human mind is the arena, and we must choose whether we are going to put our thoughts on the side of God, good, and immortal man, or on the side of animal magnetism, matter, and mortal man.

Although his addresses were strong lessons in divine metaphysics, he never lost touch with the human side of life. He recognized the problems of his students and provided the spiritual teaching to overcome them. Always he referred to the need to pray scientifically, and this address of 1935 deals with this scientific form of prayer known as the Christian Science treatment. It is obviously based upon his years of successful healing work.

The challenges of the '30s have passed into history only to be replaced by present ones just as demanding as any of the past, and because Truth is timeless, the metaphysics in this address are as relevant to our own problems as they were to those of the Great Depression. Mr. Kilpatrick's tireless devotion to the Christian Science Cause suggests that he would approve the publication of his address. It will now reach far into the future and become an inspiration to many who, like himself, are "honest seekers of Truth."

TREATMENT
Association Address of 1935

by

William D. Kilpatrick

Metaphysics may be considered to be either divine or physical. The explanation of matter in its true light may be said to be physical metaphysics. That is, today matter is being explained by many physicists as a mental phenomenon. It is being explained as a phenomenon of mortal or carnal mind, and as Christian Science has to deal with the divine Mind alone, the explanation of matter as mental may be said to be physical metaphysics. The explanation of God as All-in-all or divine Mind, and of God's creation as spiritual, may be said to be divine metaphysics.

I want to devote this discussion to the more practical feature of the application of what we have learned in Science. The letter of Christian Science is one thing. The spirit of Christian Science is another thing. "The letter killeth, but the spirit giveth life," Paul tells us. To understand what Christian Science teaches about God, man and the universe, and about matter, mortal man and the like, is a necessary foundation for demonstration. When this foundation is clearly laid so that there are no mental questionings and queries, the process of demonstrating this Truth becomes not only an easy one, but one of individual spontaneity of thought.

Demonstrating Christian Science, or Truth, means gaining a clear individual concept of the nothingness of matter and the allness of God. Demonstration is putting into active operation the truth you know about God and man. This operation is purely and exclusively individual. No one could any more tell you how to give a treatment, or how to individually arrive at the clear mental state which heals, than one could vicariously know the multiplication table for you. And, even at that, this is not a correct simile or statement, as a treatment is in no wise comparable to the recital of the multiplication table.

In fact, a treatment is quite the opposite. A treatment cannot be the parrot-like repetition of stilted phrases and metaphysical formulas. A treatment is a conviction, and not something directed at something. A treatment is the individual clear mental perception of the truth about God and man. A treatment does not involve a fixed method. Individual mental clarification of thought is never arrived at by the same route, or through the same mental processes by two different individuals. By that I mean that the clear mental conviction which might be called a treatment is not arrived at in the same way by two different people. This is something we all should be clear upon.

So many people come into class believing that class instruction will provide formulas or some secret or obscure mental method of giving treatments. Class instruction and association meetings are for the sole purpose of giving the student a clear metaphysical foundation of thought whereby firm and secure spiritual convictions may be arrived at. These firm, spiritual convictions concerning any situation with which one is confronted, constitute treatment; and these convictions are not arrived at in individual consciousness by any set rule or method of procedure. One should finish his class work with ample understanding of truth to enable him not only to do his own mental work, but which should, likewise, enable him to do any work for others that might come to him.

There is no secret or trick about giving a treatment. Many class taught students look with fear or dread or timidity on the prospect of giving a treatment, whereas the only benefit to be derived from Christian Science study and work is gaining that mental vision of Truth which enables one to scientifically meet every argument of error with which one may be confronted, either mentally or physically. Every right thought is a treatment. In fact, that is all a treatment is — *right thinking*. Everyone here is as capable of right thinking as everyone else. Everyone here is capable, this minute, of giving a treatment, because a treatment is applying what you know of Truth to the condition at hand.

Do not be mesmerized into the belief that giving a treatment is something in which only the practitioners can be instructed. Each one of us should, and I presume does, each day give himself a good treatment in Christian Science. That is what Science is for. That is what class instruction is for. Christian Science, or the operation of Truth, is not something which operates from without individual consciousness. Christian Science is just like any other science or study. The multiplication tables are worth nothing to you and me simply because someone also knows them, or they exist in books to which we may have ready access. The only use the multiplication tables are to you and me is what we know and hold of them in individual consciousness. The fact that five and five equal ten does not help you and me to work out a problem in mathematics until we know it and apply it. And so God, Truth, the Christ, Christian Science, are of no use to us until they become fixed in our consciousness.

These different things not only must become fixed in individual consciousness, but their classification and designation must become fixed in consciousness. That is, our understanding should embrace the knowledge of the difference between, or the similarity of God, the Christ, the Holy Ghost, man, the universe, etc. Do not get into the very harmful habit of thinking that because you are a Christian Scientist and have named the name of Christian Science, that fact in itself is your saviour, your protector or your salvation. God does not become God to us until we reflect Him in consciousness. God has nothing to do with matter. He has nothing to do with the mortal or carnal mind. Therefore He has nothing to do with you and me if we think we live in matter and express the carnal in thought.

* Our very first step in the demonstration of Christian Science, or in giving a treatment, lies in our clear understanding of God, and how to claim and make practical our individual indissoluble union with him. That union and its conviction are accomplished only in individual consciousness. A mortal man does not reflect God. The immortal man reflects God, and in our growth in Truth, you and I put on the immortal to just the extent that we actively and consciously reflect God. You and I reflect God, relatively speaking, through our own individual volition, and not because of God. Scientifically speaking, all there is to any of us, in reality, is our reflection of God. But to accomplish our complete disillusionment as to the material man and our existence as material beings — this operation has to be a voluntary gesture on our part. It is nothing that God can undertake to do for us. We are living in matter or illusion because of our own wrong thinking. Therefore, it is our own right thinking that will dispel the illusion of materiality. God does not voluntarily enter our consciousness, and through His own volition dispel the darkness for us. There is no darkness. We think there is. That is why individual mental effort is required to bring light, or the realization of light. This is so clearly expressed in the first chapter of John: "In the beginning was the Word, [Light] and the Word was with God, and the Word was God. The same was in the beginning with God. All things were made by him; and without him was not any thing made that was made. In him was life; and the life was the light of men. And the light shineth in darkness; and the darkness comprehended it not."

Although we are all dwelling as children of God, here and now, in the radiance of the light of Life, the work of dispelling the darkness and bringing in the light becomes individual. There is nothing in the world God can do for us. He has done it all. He is here. We dwell in Him. We are surrounded and encompassed by this light of Life, and yet our own wrong thinking has enshrouded us in the darkness of materiality. Therefore our own right thinking is the only thing that will take us out of the darkness and reveal to us the light, and therefore our own seeming progress must be through individual effort. God will never come to us. He has come. We must go to Him. We must bring Him into consciousness, actively, before we can begin to bring the light of Truth into operation and experience.

Material Existence Is in Individual Consciousness

As a man "thinketh in his heart, so is he," we read in the Book of Proverbs. Just as the man of God's creating is the expression or reflection of the one infinite Mind or intelligence which we call God, so, in its attempted counterfeit creation, the carnal mind, claiming to be one mind, just as the divine Mind is one, produces its own concept of material creation through what may be called individual expression of the carnal mind. Just as man in the image and likeness of God is the reflection of God, so the image and likeness of the carnal mind is an expression of the carnal mind. Inasmuch as God never created a carnal mind, there cannot be a carnal mind; therefore there can be no illusion and no material counterfeit.

Now that is exact. That is one of the positive convictions with which your consciousness must be imbued in giving a treatment. There is not a carnal mind. Therefore there is no counterfeit creation and no attempted counterfeit creation. Your patient, whether yourself or another, was never born. He has existed eternally in the divine consciousness without process of conception, germination, generation, birth or development. Only through understanding this fundamental fact can you reach this clear mental concept that you have nothing to heal, and that there is nothing wrong with the patient, whether the patient is yourself or another. But that is getting a little ahead of what I was going to discuss — that is, the material concept of creation.

Through understanding this claim of error or mortal mind, we can gain a clear sense of what matter is or claims to be. Anything which has to do with error, is just error, and error is nothing at all. Error has no Mind, no God, and no Principle. Now, error says that there is just one mind, and that mind is carnal, and that all minds partake of that carnal mind.

On the other hand, there is the one divine Mind, God, and all men are reflections of that one infinite Mind. To explain the situation and to point the pathway out of this mirage or illusion into the full consciousness of our real selfhood, our real state of spiritual existence as children of God, we have a third mind, or state of consciousness, which is called the *human mind* or *human consciousness*. Inasmuch as you and I are here and now perfect, spiritual ideas existing as individual entities in the divine Mind, there is actually no more reality to what is termed the *human mind* than there is to what is termed the *carnal mind*. The human mind, to sense, is a mixture, whereas the divine is pure and unadulterated. And just as the divine is pure and unadulterated, so the carnal, while not claiming to be pure, claims itself to be the one and only mind and unadulterated by the divine Mind. So, in our explanation of the illusion of material existence and our present method of escape from the illusion, we have to deal with the so-called carnal mind, the divine Mind, and the so-called human mind, or consciousness. I want to review this part of my teaching to build a foundation for what I shall discuss later on.

Keeping in mind the three states of consciousness which I have just mentioned — that is, the divine, the carnal, and the human — the process of material existence so-called and salvation therefrom, is explainable. The process of material existence does not involve the divine, but salvation from material existence does involve the divine. The material exists simply because of the supposed absence of the divine. The process of material existence involves four conditions, all included within the realm of the carnal mind or consciousness: First, there is the so-called carnal mind claiming existence as one mind outside of individual consciousness. In its claim to oneness, the carnal at the outset attempts to simulate or counterfeit the divine. Second in order comes the so-called human mind or state of consciousness, which represents your and my state of existence here and now. Third in order is the acceptance of the carnal mind into human consciousness. Fourth is the objectification of the mortal or carnal mind which our human mind has accepted or admitted into consciousness. The mortal or carnal mind does not become matter until it is admitted to and objectified by the human mind as matter.

From this it will be seen that the material world is not a creation of the carnal mind, which creation has always existed outside your and my consciousness; but it is rather *an individual state of consciousness*, and does not exist as matter outside your or my individual consciousness The use and understanding of the term *individual* is most essential in comprehending what is meant here. You and I do not become conscious of matter as something existing outside ourselves. We become individually conscious of matter because we individually create matter. Matter is not a creation of mortal mind outside your and my thinking, nor is it a creation of the aggregate consciousness of all other so-called carnal thinking of a material world of people. The world of matter in which you and I seem to live is individual, and exists in our individual experience only so long as the carnal mind exists in our individual consciousness. So do you not see that the material is entirely individual? And thus do you not see how entirely individual our salvation from the material must be? By replacing the objects of sense with the ideas of Soul, is this process accomplished. And this brings to the consciousness of each individual the millennium.

The millennium is individual entirely, because the carnal is only a mistaken concept of the individual. As material existence is an individual suppositious existence, the millennium or heaven is a universal, eternal, infinite state, and you and I reach that state of spiritual consciousness through individual spiritualization of thought only. As to the nature of material existence as an objectification of an individual consciousness, Mary Baker Eddy has said, in her definition of devil in the 'Glossary' of *Science and Health with Key to the Scriptures*: "Devil: Evil; a lie; error; neither corporeality nor mind; the opposite of Truth; a belief in sin, sickness, and death; animal magnetism or hypnotism; the lust of the flesh, which saith: 'I am life and intelligence in matter. There is more than one mind, for I am mind, — a wicked mind, self-made or created by a tribal god and put into the opposite of mind, termed matter, thence to reproduce a mortal universe, including man, not after the image and likeness of Spirit, but after its own image.'"

Here Mrs. Eddy refers to the devil as that which claims to be mind which is put into matter "thence to reproduce a mortal universe, including man," etc. That is, it is necessary that this carnal mind must be admitted into what we call brain, or matter, and this admission to the human consciousness, reproduces the material world. The latter part of this definition makes it very clear that material existence is an individual state of consciousness, or illusion, and not a universal state, self-created by the carnal mind independent of the carnal state of consciousness.

I want to impress on your thought the fact that the material universe is strictly individual and that salvation therefrom must likewise be individual. Here is a statement made by Sir James Jeans, the noted English physical scientist. Sir Jeans holds a very high position in the esteem of the English people, as well as throughout the world, and his views along any line of thought are held as authority by most people who think in terms of the material. He says: "The old physics imagined it was studying the objective nature (matter) which had its own existence independently of the mind which perceived it — which, indeed, had existed from all eternity whether it was perceived or not." Of the new physics he goes on to say, "The nature (matter) we study does not consist so much of something we perceive as of our perceptions. It is not the object of the subject-object relation, but the relation itself."

From all of these various standpoints we find ourselves gradually converging at one clear understanding that the material universe is an individual illusion and not a collective one. And to the extent that you can clearly perceive that matter is an illusion, will you be able to heal the sick.

The Hundred Percent of Consciousness

To continue a little farther, the human mind, which we have found is capable of including within itself both carnal and divine precepts, constitutes our present state of existence. The human mind, or human consciousness, is what you and I are. It is what constitutes our world, our surroundings, our material embodiment, everything capable of being conceived of through the senses of seeing, feeling, tasting, smelling, and hearing. The carnal, which is contained in, and constitutes, and contributes to our sense of matter or material existence, is what Mrs. Eddy has termed *animal magnetism*. I shall dwell on that at length a little further along, but, just briefly, in reply to the query as to what animal magnetism is, it may be described as all that we can see, feel, taste, hear and smell materially. Animal magnetism is not a force or a process. It is an illusion.

Now, this human mind, which is capable of receiving or rejecting either the divine or the carnal, constitutes your and my one hundred percent of existence. All that you and I know, or are conscious of — either the divine or the carnal or both — constitutes our existence. All that we are conscious of — either good or bad — both combined, constitute one hundred percent. This one hundred percent is all we are conscious of, or ever will be conscious of, in any way shape or form, either spiritually or materially. This one hundred percent in each individual consciousness differs. Some of us may include more of error than others; some more Truth than others. So each individual one hundred percent differs from every other individual one hundred percent.

Now, it is the percentage of the carnal which exists in our individual consciousness that constitutes our material world. We accept the carnal into thought, and this carnal in thought, or consciousness, is in turn objectified as matter. Inasmuch as the amount and variety of either the carnal or the divine which we hold in consciousness, depends entirely on our own individual volition; inasmuch as we may individually accept or reject the carnal or the divine in proportion to suit our own will, it can be seen how we hold within our grasp the key to every situation. We can see how individual our salvation is. No one else makes or creates our human consciousness for us. We do that ourselves, and we regulate the proportion of the good or bad which that consciousness entertains. It is all up to us. No one else creates our consciousness. No one else does our thinking for us. No one but our own selves can put into our consciousness any carnal thought or any divine idea, and no one can eject these from our consciousness. God provides divine ideas, but you and I admit them into consciousness at our own will. The devil or evil provides carnal thoughts, and you and I accept or reject them just as we please. So the one hundred percent which constitutes our individual consciousness is made up of a certain percentage of carnal and a certain percentage of divine.

The carnal which is voluntarily held in our individual consciousness, constitutes our material existence, our material environment, our material embodiment, etc. So if our body seems full of misery, pain or sickness, where do we look for the cause? Also where do we look for the remedy? If our material picture is cluttered up with lack, limitation, unhappiness, poverty, inharmony and the like, where do we look for the cause, and where do we look for the remedy? We look for the remedy within. Who puts sickness into our bodies, and lack and limitation into our experiences? No one but ourselves. The divine must first be admitted to human consciousness before we can look for relief from any of our ills, and thus does relief from these ills come from within, although the divine is outside of man as one infinite Mind. The ideas which emanate from the one infinite divine Mind must be admitted into consciousness before that consciousness can create a better universe.

To quote one citation from *Science and Health* in connection with this: "The human mind acts more powerfully to offset the discords of matter and the ills of the flesh, in proportion as it puts less weight into the material or fleshly scale and more weight into the spiritual scale."

The "material or fleshly scale" naturally refers to the carnal mind because, as Mrs. Eddy tells us, "matter and mortal mind are one," and "the spiritual scale" naturally refers to the divine Mind. So it becomes clear that Mrs. Eddy recognized that the human mind represents and includes the full extent of error which manifests itself in our everyday existence, and she also recognized and taught that only as the divine is admitted into consciousness can existence, and especially the human body, be freed from its bondage of carnal beliefs. And thus does the individual human mind include all of individual existence, either good or bad.

The human mind, as we have said, constitutes the one hundred percent of individual existence. This one hundred percent is composed of a very large percentage of the carnal and a very small percentage of the divine — especially small before we have become interested in Christian Science. The amount and variety of true thought which we have thus far admitted into human consciousness is but an infinitesimal percentage of that which will be unfolded and revealed to us as we progress in our study and understanding of Christian Science.

All there is to existence, either spiritual or material, is consciousness. There is no matter except in a supposititious, mortal consciousness, and spiritual existence is divine consciousness. God never created or recognized any other than the divine. Therefore there is no material consciousness, and, in reality, no material concept of a material consciousness — or matter. And this is the point upon which rests all your success in healing — your ability to clearly perceive that there is no matter. It is easy enough to assert that there is no matter. It is easy enough to repeat indefinitely the 'Scientific Statement of Being' as found in our textbook; but the mere repetition of those statements will get us nowhere in healing the sick. It is the clear spiritual perception of the nothingness of matter as a fact, and not as a theory, that heals. In *Science and Health* Mrs. Eddy writes: "A belief in Truth is better than a belief in error," and is it possible that the reason we do not heal the sick as readily and as instantaneously as we should is that we are entertaining only a "belief in Truth"?

A Belief in Truth

A belief in Truth, is, of course, desirable. A belief in Truth is an essential in the understanding of Truth, but a mere belief in Truth will never heal the sick. We may believe that "there is no life, truth, intelligence nor substance in matter," but unless we understand that there is none and perceive this clearly, to the complete exclusion in our individual consciousness of matter even as a possibility, our efforts at healing will go for naught. And this consciousness of the nothingness of matter and the allness of Spirit is not a long, drawn-out process. The consciousness of Truth is an instantaneous thing, and the momentary consciousness of Truth in any condition is all that is required to heal. A long, protracted, involved mental argument is not necessary to bring about that spiritual consciousness which heals, although few of us have as yet arrived at the stage of consciousness where this clear realization is constantly with us.

In *Science and Health* Mrs. Eddy writes: "One moment of divine consciousness, or the spiritual understanding of Life and Love, is a foretaste of eternity. This exalted view, obtained and retained when the Science of being is understood, would bridge over with life discerned spiritually the interval of death, and man would be in the full consciousness of his immortality and eternal harmony, where sin, sickness, and death are unknown." This "one moment of divine consciousness" will also enable you and me to heal the sick instantaneously, and this is not a far off prospect or possibility. It is a present condition which may be obtained here and now. In fact, it is a condition of consciousness which is absolutely necessary to successfully cope with disease, either in oneself or in others.

Let's go back a little to the one hundred percent of consciousness. As I stated, each individual consciousness — that is, your and my thinking — constitutes our existence, our environment, our experience, our home, our family, our acquaintances, our very being. Nothing exists outside consciousness, and our world is material or spiritual in the degree that the carnal or divine hold place in our individual consciousness. So our one hundred percent of individual consciousness may be composed of, we will say, by way of example, ninety-five percent carnal thinking and five percent divine. As the divine increases in our consciousness the carnal diminishes. Both cannot increase at the same time, nor can both diminish at the same time. Consciousness always remains at one hundred percent. If the percentage of carnal increases in individual consciousness the divine is bound to decrease to just that extent. If the divine increases in individual consciousness the carnal decreases just that much.

Individual Salvation

From this explanation, we can begin to understand the real process of individual salvation. The thinking of no one else on the face of this earth can constitute our individual consciousness or any part of it. Someone else could sit down from morning until night and try to think for you, but he could not change your individual consciousness one iota. You, and only you, can bring about any change in your consciousness. If your and my consciousness is wholly one hundred percent material or carnal, we are then completely devoid of spirituality, and we are conscious of nothing but the material. But when we begin to include a little of the truth in our thinking, then our universe, our surroundings, our home, our business, etc., begin to lose some of the carnal which constitutes our thinking, and the spiritual which we have taken into consciousness replaces just that much of the carnal in our universe, our surroundings, our home and our business, because what you and I perceive through the medium of our physical senses is simply an index to or the objectification of our thinking. Our body — our physical body — is a state of thought. It is not a state of matter. It is the individual objectification of our individual thinking, and consequently represents and includes just and only what we have admitted into thought. In *The People's Idea of God* Mrs. Eddy has written: "We possess our own body, and make it harmonious or discordant according to the images that thought reflects upon it. The emancipation of our bodies from sickness will follow mind's freedom from sin; and, as St. Paul admonishes, we should be waiting for the adoption, to wit, the redemption of our body. The feeblest mind, enlightened and spiritualized, can free its body from disease as well as sin. . . . Mortals, *alias* mortal minds, make the laws that govern their bodies, as directly as men pass legislative acts and enact penal codes; while the body, obedient to the legislation of mind, but ignorant of the law of belief, calls its own enactments 'laws of matter.'"

Then in *Science and Health* Mrs. Eddy writes: "Note how thought makes the face pallid. It either retards the circulation or quickens it, causing a pale or flushed cheek. In the same way thought increases or diminishes the secretions, the action of the lungs, of the bowels, and of the heart. The muscles, moving quickly or slowly and impelled or palsied by thought, represent the action of all the organs of the human system, including brain and viscera."

A few years ago such statements as we have just heard from the pen of Mrs. Eddy would have met with derision and scoffs from the physical scientists; but today most of the prominent physical scientists of the world are repeating the same fundamental facts as deductions arrived at from their own material reasoning. Dr. George Crile, the noted physician and surgeon of Cleveland, Ohio, has written: "Worry kills man. Fear kills man. Hate kills man. Jealousy kills man. Man doesn't do these things with his intellect; he worries, fears, hates and is jealous with his organs. Man must learn on peril of death, to intellectualize his fears and emotions. No longer do plagues kill man — infections and emotions do this job. Man must learn how to rest; the perpetual worrier in this high speed age faces physical ill-health. Emotions — love, hate, fear, jealousy — are but stimulating processes, loosing currents of electricity through certain paths. Now, this, in simple terms, means that emotions let loose are like supercharges of electricity — they use up the previous energy of man; they destroy and in the end they can kill."

The effects of fear, worry, etc., on the body were brought to light and emphasized years ago by Mrs. Eddy, and it is only through the education of thought incident to her teachings that we are today getting a confirmation of her spiritual deductions from our physical science brothers. The remedy, then, for the ills of the flesh, which are caused by our emotions or wrong thinking, is evident. The remedy is patently right thinking. Mrs. Eddy has met the situation in one statement where she says in *Science and Health*, "Divine Love always has met and always will meet every human need." This statement of Mrs. Eddy's is frequently met with the question, "If Divine Love has always met every human need" what about all the lack, the misery, the want and the poverty which confront us on all sides today?

The Need for Love

Many times I have been confronted with the question from patients, "Why are not my needs for money, health, food, clothing, etc., met, if Divine Love always meets these things? I owe everybody from the butcher and the baker to the candlestick maker. I am sick most of the time. I have no home, etc." Every practitioner in Christian Science is confronted with that wail of helplessness from the lips of the sick and needy. It is not easy to convince those who are in conditions of distress that their own wrong thinking is the cause of their difficulties, no matter how free they may be from evil intent or motive. The answer to any query of that kind is simply, of course, that the patient has not been a channel for divine Love.

The only reason anyone is sick or poverty stricken is because he is not conscious of Love. Sickness and poverty are states of consciousness and not conditions of matter. They are not persons, places or things; they are states of consciousness, conditions of thought. They are the supposed absence of Divine Mind in thought. While Divine Mind is always in the thought of man, yet the belief that this Mind is *not* in our thoughts makes it possible for us to be conscious of the belief of lack and sickness. The very moment we begin actively and consciously to express in thought the Divine Mind, just then does the Divine Mind begin to meet every human need. In reality, there never has been any human need, and as we begin to admit the Divine Mind into thought, we begin to see that fact clearly, and as we see that fact clearly, then does it appear to us in consciousness that "Divine Love always has met and always will meet every human need." When we can clearly see that there is no human need to be met, just then are our human needs met.

Remember that there is nothing relative in Christian Science. There is no good, better, best. The relative exists in the carnal consciousness only. There is just infinite perfection here and now. That is your basis for thought and demonstration. Never consider your patient in the light of a material being. The concept of him as a material personality is his mistake — not yours. It is your clear concept of him that enables you to relieve him of the result of his wrong thinking. Remember that Jesus never healed anyone without making it clear to them that the permanency of their healing rested entirely with them. Almost invariably he said to them that their future welfare of their being rested with them. He said, to paraphrase his statement in several instances, "Now, I have healed you this time. But whether you stay healed depends on you." In other words, "Go and sin no more lest a worse thing come upon you."

Carnal and Divine Consciousness

So this one hundred percent which constitutes our thinking is composed largely of the carnal. This carnal includes all the matter of which we are conscious; all the evil of which we are conscious; all the inharmony of which we are conscious; all the sickness of which we are conscious. As we begin to learn something of Christian Science, and thus begin to take into our consciousness something of the divine, the proportion of the carnal is decreased to the extent that the divine is admitted, and thus we begin to acquire what Mrs. Eddy has termed "a better belief." Our consciousness includes our belief of material embodiment. All there is to our bodies is thought — nothing else. And it is individual thought — our own individual thinking — which is responsible for our material embodiment. The same individual consciousness which includes and has created a material body also includes and creates individual sickness, inharmony, and the like.

Now, with the influx of the divine into individual consciousness, just that much of the carnal is thrust out, and the divine takes its place. If there is enough of Truth admitted to consciousness to completely eliminate the belief of sickness which has dominated our thinking, then we have a consciousness devoid of sickness; and if consciousness is devoid of sickness, then the objectifications of that consciousness — that is, the material body, etc. — becomes devoid of sickness, and as a result we have a material body free from the claim of sickness. The same would apply to poverty, sorrow, inharmony, and the like.

So our material world begins to improve under the regimen of right thinking, and while our material concepts are not more spiritual than they were before, they are less material. That is, a well body is no more spiritual because of truth in consciousness than it ever was, but it may be less material. Matter and Spirit, Mrs. Eddy tells us, never co-mingle. No matter can ever become spiritualized. Matter simply becomes nothing in the sunlight of Truth. It might be said that matter becomes dematerialized through the application of Truth to thought. As there is no matter, it can be readily seen that salvation is purely a process of educating the human mind, by the influx of Truth, out of its belief in matter and into the understanding of the allness of Spirit; and when this is done completely, then there is no matter. So we have to deal entirely with thought, and never with matter. And through this process of elimination is the process of spiritualization and salvation accomplished.

Gaining a Better Understanding of Treatment

In your work in Christian Science, in your work in treating, healing and even teaching (because the dissemination of Truth by any means involves teaching), *your basic premise is God.* Nothing can be accomplished in any direction in Christian Science without a clear and workable understanding of God. The farther I go in the study and practice of this great Truth, the greater appears to me the necessity of knowing God, and realizing just what He is and what He means in my thinking and my work. In *Science and Health* Mrs. Eddy has given us the definition of God. She has, in fact, given us several definitions, and has devoted much time and space to the explanation of Him. She answers the question, What is God?, with this definition: "God is incorporeal, divine, supreme, infinite Mind, Spirit, Soul, Principle, Life, Truth, Love." And in the 'Glossary' she defines God as "The great I AM; the all-knowing, all-seeing, all-acting, all-wise, all-loving, and eternal; Principle; Mind; Soul; Spirit; Life; Truth; Love; all substance; intelligence."

But with God clearly defined, the vital, demonstrable and workable understanding of Him must still have to come through our own consciousness. Just to read and understand what these definitions of God mean, in a mere academic fashion, will not accomplish a great deal. I can hardly explain to you in words what has come to me in my contemplation and silent mental work by way of unfoldment and clear conviction concerning the real nature and import of God, and yet I know that I have but glimpsed the beauty, the grandeur, the sublimity and the wonders of His greatness which are here for all of us to perceive and partake of, whenever our clear consciousness will allow its entrance. The more I work in Christian Science and the more I endeavor to put into practice and demonstration what I have already gained therefrom, the more I am convinced that it is our clear concept of God, and God only, that will enable us to instantaneously and completely heal the sick, cast out demons and raise the dead.

In our work in Science, in our treatments for others, in our daily work for ourselves, the contemplation of God is what will bring the desired results. Nothing can be done in a Christian Science treatment without a firm foundation based upon a clear concept of God. The nothingness of matter can never become clear in our consciousness until we have gained a clear concept of God. All of the arguments which you mentally employ in your work in Science must be predicated on your concept of God, and unless your concept of God is clear, your arguments and your treatments will not be effective. I am convinced that the clearer one gets as to God alone, the less he will have to employ the argumentative type of treatment. You and I have not yet arrived at that stage in our understanding where we will not for some time need to affirm and deny in our treatments, but I do know that as we advance in our understanding and practice of this truth, the less we will rely on the argument in our treatments and the more we will depend on our clear concept of God. The clearer we become in thought as to the real nature and import of God, the better and more certain become the result and outcome of our treatment. The time will come, perhaps has come in a degree, in the experience of many of us, when the contemplation of God, and God alone, will constitute our only conscious treatment. As we grow in the understanding and application of Christian Science, the greater becomes the all-inclusiveness of the understanding of God in consciousness. That is, the clearer we become as to what God really is, His infinitude, His allness, His creativeness, His present and only being, the clearer and more certain we become in our treatments.

And let me impress upon you the necessity and value of daily work in Christian Science. Never neglect your daily work and reading because of lack of time, the pressure of business, the urge of household duties, social duties, etc. You will find, as most of you have found, that there is nothing gained in Christian Science vicariously, and that if God is to be with you in your business, in your home and in your daily associations, you have got to make Him a conscious presence by your pure and right thinking. You cannot avail yourselves of the assistance of God simply by depending on His presence and not including Him in your consciousness.

Sometimes, as I said before, I hear the statement from class taught students that they do not understand how to give a treatment, not even for themselves. Class teaching is for the purpose of enabling you to give a correct treatment, and if one has emerged from class without enough understanding of truth to enable him to do his own mental work as well as work for others, if required, it is too bad for the student and too bad for the teacher.

A treatment, as I have many times explained, is not something which anyone can tell you how to give. You have to give your own treatments out of the spontaneity of Truth in your own consciousness. A treatment is simply knowing the truth. No one can tell you how to know the truth; but a teacher can tell you what the truth is, and it is your own knowing of that truth that constitutes a treatment. A clear concept of God is a treatment. It is the best treatment you can give. The clearer you get as to God, the better your treatment will be. You will find that the time you spend in your study of Christian Science and in giving yourself a treatment each day is not time taken from your business, your work and your home duties. The time devoted to daily reading and mental work is never lost, and always results in more time for business, more time for home and work, etc. The time devoted to daily mental work and study simply coordinates your daily material duties, orders them in accord with divine law and harmony, and makes everything work out to so much better advantage than it would were you to start the day without this work and study. Clear thinking is bound to be manifest in clear acting and orderly and harmonious material existence; and the more time one spends on study and work, the more orderly and harmonious become his daily duties. The power of a well ordered mentality is always manifested in a well ordered and harmonious daily material routine.

Now, anyone, as I said, can give a treatment, and if you will make it a practice each day to sit down and just know the truth for yourself which you have learned from Christian Science, you will soon find how easy it is to give yourself a treatment, and how little labor and confusion is involved in the process.

The first thing in any treatment is *God*, and, as I said, the clearer you get as to God and His true nature the better will be your treatment. Anyone here can sit down and close his eyes for a few moments and think on God. The thought thus devoted to the contemplation of God is a treatment. A treatment is simply the activity of Truth in consciousness, and this Truth in your consciousness will furnish you all that it is necessary for you to know to meet any given manifestation or argument of error. One will never learn how to give a treatment until he tries. A treatment is individual. A treatment is individual because existence is individual. If you and I were all existing here in this material state as a result of one well defined and outlined and omnipotent general plan of material existence; if we were all existing in our material states as the objects of one infinite creator who has fashioned and molded us materially from one infinite and complete plan of existence, then we could formulate and put into practice one set of treatments or particular forms of treatment for our ills. But this is not so. Such individual material existence is the outcome of an individual consciousness. To be sure, each individual material consciousness is the conscious expression of a mortal or carnal mind which claims to exist as one mind outside of individual consciousness, and which is manifested or expressed individually at the will and volition of the individual.

If you and I had no volition in our method of thinking, if we did not have the individual ability to accept or reject the carnal at our own wills, then we could formulize our treatments and have them all conform to one set method or mode. But as we voluntarily control our own consciousness, and as our material existence is the objectified manifestation of this individual consciousness, we can see how thoroughly individual our treatments must be, because we have nothing to deal with except our own individual illusions or misconceptions, and not the illusions or misconceptions of another's thinking. If you and I knew and clearly comprehended all that there is to know about God, we would ascend as did Jesus at the time of his disappearance from mortal vision. Any of us can start out in our efforts to give a treatment by knowing the definition of God which Mrs. Eddy has given us in the 'Glossary' of *Science and Health*, and in 'Recapitulation.' From this basis must emanate all of the convictions upon which we can deny the error and affirm the truth. *There is no claim of error in the consciousness of mankind that cannot be met by understanding what God is.*

The different synonyms of God with which Mrs. Eddy has provided us, give us the foundation upon which every claim of error can be met and mastered. So do you not see how necessary it is to dwell on God in your treatments? To speak for myself, I can say that most of my treatments consist on contemplating God. I find that the clearer I get as to understanding God, the more often I return to Him in my treatment. It almost seems to me at times that if I allow myself, in my treatments, to get into the intricacies and the enigmas which mortal mind presents, I just have to flee back mentally to God as a sort of refuge and sure fortress in making my treatment the powerful and omnipotent thing which a treatment should be.

Many cases of mortal mind involve so much of error and so much confusion and obscuration that, unless we watch, we become involved in our treatments in the very error which we are trying to heal, and in that case our only refuge is to hurry back to God to get away from it all, lest our skirts become tainted with the very thing we are trying to unsee. The more I get into the study and application of Christian Science, the more I dwell in and contemplate on God. It is difficult to get into the intricacies of error and not get smeared ourselves, and I find that, in my treatments when I allow myself to get too far afield in trying to make the application of my treatment fit the particular error at hand in all its forms, my only refuge is God. There is a great temptation in giving a treatment to get involved ourselves in the error which we are trying to overcome; and when we find that we have ventured too far, our refuge, our relief, our hope, lies in getting ourselves, our patient, and our thoughts back into God just as fast as we can.

Understanding God Destroys Error

It is a little difficult to express to you in words just what I am trying to impress on you, but those of you who have been in the work of healing will understand what I mean when I say that our haven of rest, our sure defense from the errors which we are trying in our treatments to heal, lies in our consciousness of God. Our whole object in giving a treatment is to unsee error — to dematerialize man and the universe — and we cannot do that if we allow ourselves, in our treatments, to get so far away from God that we can see nothing but the error. In giving a treatment, do not fall into the trap which mortal mind sets for us by trying to hook up your treatment with the error at hand. Do not attempt to make your treatment apply to the error to be corrected. This will confuse you, and get you into matter and error up to your ears. This is a very common error with students, and it is one which will always result from the mental practice of endeavoring to hook up a spiritual idea with a material concept. There is no material concept, and therefore there can be no spiritual idea of that which does not exist. Forget it. Forget the material concept and deal exclusively with spiritual ideas, and you will never become confused.

Not long ago I got a letter from a student who said that he could get just about so far in a treatment; but when it came to the point of applying the treatment to the trouble at hand, he was sunk. This error of trying, ourselves, to make the application of the truth of our treatments to the errors of mortal mind is a most disastrous one. "But," someone may ask, "how is one going to make a treatment effective if it is not applied to the error?" That is a righteous question, but the answer is that the treatment itself, the truth itself, makes its own application. We cannot make the application without agreeing with the error. Our whole aim in a Christian Science treatment is to unsee and get rid of the error in our individual consciousness, and if we make an individual mental effort to apply our treatments to that which we have been trying to realize as nothing, we are then confusing our treatments and making a reality of that which we would see as unreal. George Shaw Cook, in an article from the *Christian Science Sentinel*, states: "Truth is its own utterance, its own impulsion." "Truth is its own impulsion" — that is putting it succinctly and clearly. We, individually, do not make the application of our treatments. The treatments make their own application, and thus all you and I have to do in giving a treatment is to know the truth and unsee the error, and the application is then self-consummated. To repeat further from Mr. Cook's article: "Truth is its own utterance, its own impulsion. It is irresistible: nothing can withstand it. Nothing can obstruct, hinder, delay or limit its activity. Nothing can reverse its affirmations or their effect. Nothing can limit its capacity for expression. It is, in fact, the Word of God, which, the prophet Isaiah has declared, 'shall not return unto me [God] void, but it shall accomplish that which I please, and it shall prosper in the thing whereunto I sent it.'"

Now, it is not the mere repetition of these words which accomplishes these results. Simply mentally to repeat the statement, "Nothing can obstruct, hinder, delay or limit this treatment," as a sort of a command or challenge, will never lend the unction to a treatment which a clear understanding of what you are saying will give. You do not make these affirmations to scare away opposition or compel error to flee away. These statements should be made as the result of the conviction that there is no obstruction, hindrance or delay either mental or material in existence. A treatment is not designed to establish a new order of things. It is for the purpose of revealing the old order, the true, the original order of things. You do not have to make a treatment work. All you have to do is to let it work. Don't stand in the way of your treatment.

Treatment Defined

A treatment is not something you have created, developed, evolved or promulgated. A treatment is the mental statement of a fact which has existed from time immemorial. A treatment is something distinctly separate and apart from the one giving the treatment. No treatment is your treatment. It is God's. It is Truth expressed, and Truth expressed is God expressed, and because it is God expressed, it is, for that very reason, omnipotent and infinite. Truth is infinite. A treatment is a statement of Truth, and therefore a treatment is infinite, and because a treatment is infinite, and because it is an expression of Truth, and because all Truth is here and now and everywhere, there is no belief of distance, time, place or separation that can interfere with a treatment. Truth does not eliminate time, space and distance. It eliminates the *belief* of time, space and distance, and it is only the belief of these things that needs to be eliminated. Understanding of the universal nature, the infinite nature of God, or good, eliminates the belief of time, distance and space. Every argument of the carnal mind can be handled and met by the use of some part of Mrs. Eddy's definition of God. By realizing the infinity of Truth, by using the qualifying adjective *infinite* as applied to God in Mrs. Eddy's definition, you do away with distance or separation in case of absent treatments.

A treatment is a thing of God, and if it is a thing of God, it must partake of all the qualities of God. And by understanding this, we endow our treatments with the omnipotence which we should attach to them, and at the same time, we relieve ourselves of any sense of personal responsibility or credit in the giving of a treatment. Personal or individual responsibility on the part of a practitioner in giving a treatment, will rob the treatment of that unction which your clear spiritual understanding of it will give. So, to gain a clear spiritual understanding of God (not an academic one) as explained in Mrs. Eddy's definition of God, is a necessary prerequisite to the successful practice of Christian Science. Remember that every claim of error can and must be handled from the broad basis of your clear understanding of God. In giving a treatment I invariably depend upon every synonym of God to clarify my thinking in connection with the case. I almost invariably apply, spiritually, each synonym of God to my patient before I can proceed to direct my mental arguments to the condition at hand. It is always well, at the beginning of a treatment, to attempt to spiritually or mentally visualize a Mind or intelligence which fills all space, and which might be said to be responsible for its own existence; a Mind which, because of its infinity, recognizes no other existence, and in which there is in reality no other existence. This Mind is self-existent consciousness and includes only that which it itself creates. Applying to this concept of Mind or intelligence the qualifying adjectives "incorporeal, divine, supreme, infinite," we completely rid our own consciousness of any sense of corporeality or material embodiment as attached to God, any sense of the carnal mind, any sense of a lesser intelligence, and any sense of a localized God. Through our mental use of the term *incorporeal* we do away with any sense of a God of material outline or confinements. To do away with any sense of God as embodied or circumscribed, and to get a clear sense of God, we must avoid any attempt to pattern our concept of God after our concept of mortal sin.

The terms which Mrs. Eddy has used in her definitions of God meet and nullify the human arguments and concepts attributed to mortal man. Mortal man is corporeal in his own estimation. God is incorporeal. Therefore, there is no similarity at that point. Mortal man is human to his own sense. God is divine and does not partake of the carnal at any point. Therefore anything that might be attributed to mortal man as human is handled by the adjective *divine* in Mrs. Eddy's definition of God. Note how the definition of God reverses mortal man's concept of man, or of himself. In the term *human* you may include a multitude of mortal mind's assertions. Under the term *human* comes the claim of human nature. And there is something I seldom fail to use in a treatment — *human nature*. It is the basis and excuse for more error than you can imagine. Under the term *human* comes all human relationships, heredity, family traits and characteristics of both mind and body, mother love, parental concern and anxiety, excuse for condoning error on the ground that one is still human. One might go on indefinitely listing the various qualities of thought which could be listed under the one word *human*. All of these are handled finally and completely by the term *divine* in the definition of God. And thus, do you not see that by applying that part of the definition of God in your understanding to the particular phases of error in your patient which this term *divine* meets, you are handling these errors on a scientific and holy basis?

In the realm of the material, all is relative. There are minds many. There are what we call good minds and better minds, evil minds and pure minds, strong minds and weak minds, spiritual minds and perverted minds. Everything in the realm of the material is relative. There is a multiplicity of everything so that no two things are alike in any material condition of thought. There is always the comparative, the relative. This is all handled and met in Mrs. Eddy's definition of God in the word *supreme*. This term *supreme*, in this instance, means *only*. So that in the realm of the spiritual, in the realm of Mind, or Life, or Love, or the other words which Mrs. Eddy has used as synonyms of God, there is nothing else. There is no lesser mind. There is no lesser life. There is no lesser love, etc. There is but the one Mind. And as man is the expression of this one Mind, do you not see how all of these terms, all of these qualifying terms used by Mrs. Eddy in connection with her definition of God, apply also to man in God's image and likeness?

Herein lies the great help which the clear spiritual understanding of the definition of God gives us in meeting the claims which mortal man would confront us with. There is no mortal man. The only man there is, is the man which is like the God which is explained in Mrs. Eddy's definition of God. Always cling to that. Always strive for that clear mental state which enables you to perceive that there is no material man because man is like God, and an infinite Mind which is self-existent and which is infinite, could not create or include the ability to create or to recreate anything lesser than Himself. God which shines by reflection could not be reflected in something that God could not Himself conceive of. Mortal man conceives himself to be an individual, finite expression. He dwells in matter. He is circumscribed. He is outlined. He rests in place and travels through space from place to place. He is conceived in restriction; he is germinated in limitation; he is born of matter and material parenthood, and his birth, his growth and his maturity all require time.

All of this is handled in Mrs. Eddy's definition of God by the various adjectives used therein, and most of these are handled especially by the term *infinite*, the last of the qualifying terms in the definition given us in the chapter on 'Recapitulation' in *Science and Health*. The term *infinite*, completely does away with any sense of limitation, locality, time, space, or process of construction. In contemplating man, never connect your patient with his mortal mind's concept of man. In fact, never think of this pile of flesh and blood and bones which calls itself a patient. That is not what you are trying to heal. You are trying to heal your concept of man as material, and you cannot do that while you think that you have a material patient, or even while you think you have any patient. There never was a patient. There never was a sick man. There never was a healer. There never was a practitioner. There never was anything to be healed.

Now, we have just touched on some of the high points regarding the adjectives in Mrs. Eddy's definition of God. Besides these we have the synonyms: Mind, Spirit, Soul, Principle, Life,

Truth, Love. Remember that man is the reflection of God, and that therefore the more you know about God, the more you can confidently affirm concerning man. And what you know about God and His reflection, man, is the healing Christ in your consciousness. It is not the mechanical argument which you employ that heals. It is the Christ which lies behind your mental argument that heals. Therefore you do not do the healing. Applying all the adjectives which we have just recited to the term *Mind* in our definition, we have taken away from the sense of Mind all that applies to mortal man as the opposite of those adjectives.

Now, to arrive at a workable and demonstrable consciousness of God in your work of healing, does not require all the time and effort which we have taken here to explain it. If it did, a treatment would be quite a laborious thing. But through a clear perception of God, this clear consciousness comes spontaneously and easily. The conviction of God as Mind, and man as the image and likeness of Mind, becomes a constant, clear, spontaneous consciousness which is ever with you, and which, as time goes on, requires less time and mental effort for its realization.

Visualizing God's Universe and Man

Imagine, if you can, a universe without any matter in it, without material persons in it, without material atmosphere, without material laws of limitation, of sickness, of gravitation, of material force of any name or nature; without any sin or carnality in it, without any hate or malice or revenge; where no one is ever born and no one ever dies, where there is no time, nor place, nor space, nor distance; where there is no process of creation; where everything is complete and has been complete throughout all time; where nothing is constructed; where there is no process of construction or development; where there is no material or physical growth; where transportation is an operation of consciousness and not a condition of matter; where there is no recreation, no pro-creation, no counterfeit creation; where there is no lack or limitation; where abundance reigns and supply is not the result of effort, but an eternal fact; where love reigns supreme and the brotherhood of man is a forever reality.

Imagine this harmonious universe, if you can, created, governed and controlled by one infinite Mind or intelligence, a Mind which knows all, sees all, comprehends all, is conscious of everything in this universe of Spirit, and which is the Father and Mother of that universe.

Imagine this all-knowing intelligence governing and pervading this universe with unerring certainty and precision, with love, with discernment, with benevolence and light.

Imagine this universe with but one Mind in it, and everything in this universe an idea of this all-knowing, all-seeing, all-acting, all-wise intelligence.

Imagine this universe without any other mind but this one divine intelligence, and the ideas of this intelligence conscious of and expressing no other Mind, and consequently a universe wherein there are not minds many, wills many, or purposes many; where the one Mind reigns supreme and everything in that universe operates in accord with this one all knowing intelligence; where there are no differing opinions, no disagreements, no quarrels, no responsibility resting on any individual in that universe; where all responsibility rests in this one infinite intelligence, and where there is no misunderstanding or difference of opinions, because there are no differing opinions; where everything in this universe is an expression of this one Mind, and no one has mentally to labor or think for himself; where everything is an involuntary expression of the harmony and peace of this one Mind.

Imagine this universe where there are no material or artificial channels of illumination; where the light of this one Mind is the only light there is, and in which is no darkness, no night and no oblivion; where the sun, the moon and the stars no longer furnish light, but where this ever-present light illumines eternally, without cessation, hindrance or uncertainty.

Imagine this universe filled with and expressing one infinite, eternal Life; a universe where everything in it is the outgrowth and expression of this one infinite Life; where there is but one Life and nothing in this universe has any life separate from this one infinite Life; where the beings in that universe have no life of their own, hence have no life to lose; where Life is not subject to matter, laws of matter, laws of heredity, laws of astrology, laws of *materia medica*, laws of nature, laws of anatomy or physiology.

Imagine this universe filled with and expressing one Truth, which Truth fills all space and which has no opposite; which Truth is expressed by everything within the realm of this perfect spiritual universe, and wherein is no error of any name or nature; where the very presence of Truth precludes the presence of any opposite condition, or error; where there are no obstacles to Truth, no matter, no mortal mind, no superstition, no ignorance, no mist, no illusion, no dream, and no darkness; where this Truth fills and illumines the universe with ever-present light and joy and peace and assurance; where this Truth dispels the possibility of fear, or a mind which can fear or thinks fear, or which thinks there is fear; where "nothing is hidden that shall not be revealed"; where there are no conflicting elements, no opposing conditions, no different methods or *modus operandi*; where harmony reigns supreme.

Imagine, if you can, this universe of Mind peopled with spiritual ideas and nothing else; where all these ideas exist in all places, at all times, and in countless numbers; where every idea is in its right place, and where every idea is coordinated and synchronized with every other idea under the supervision of this one infinite Mind which knows all its own ideas, and which governs them all with unerring certainty and precision; where all the ideas of this one Mind are governed by and subject to this one divine Mind only, and where one idea is not dependent on or out of harmony with any other idea; where all ideas are spiritual, and hence express the one infinite Mind, or Spirit, which fills all space, which is everywhere present, and which is conscious of no opposite or material existence.

Imagine this universe of spiritual ideas as the spontaneous outcome of this one all-knowing, all-seeing, all-wise, all-loving intelligence or Mind, Spirit, and Life, governed and correlated by the one creative Principle which admits of no lesser creation, no limited creation, no counterfeit creation, and no material creation.

Imagine all of these as created by or the outcome of one infinite, divine Principle, without a counterfeit or an element of competition, free from adulteration, or foreign or material influences, where no mortal mind is known or exists; where there is nothing but one divine Principle governing all these ideas in perfect harmony, peace, and love.

Imagine, if you can, all this vast universe of ideas which are the outcome and expression of this one infinite Mind, this one infinite Principle, this one infinite Truth, this one all-inclusive Life, being conscious and expressive of nothing but Mind and Life and Truth and Principle which constitutes the very Soul of these ideas.

Imagine, if you can, all this vast creation of ideas as being expressive of and enfolded in one infinite divine Love which goes to make up this Mind, this Principle, this Life, this Spirit, and this Soul.

Imagine all of these ideas as expressive of, and conscious of, no other Mind, no other Principle, no other Life, no other Spirit, no other Soul, no other Love.

Imagine all of this vast aggregation of ideas, which are governed by one Principle, one Mind, one Truth, one Life and one Love, as children of God, and imagine yourself as one of these ideas, free from the bondage or influence of matter, laws of matter, physical body, physical forms, mortal mind, birth, growth, maturity, death, and the like, and you will then have a clear demonstrable and provable sense of man as the image and likeness of God, and you will heal the sick. It is this clear sense of true spiritual existence, free from any taint of materiality, material existence, mortal mind or physicality which heals the sick.

Vision Essential to Healing

It is the absence of the possibility of error in your consciousness which enables you to heal. You cannot, for a moment, admit the possibility of a material creation or a sick patient; otherwise your treatment becomes relative or involved in error. Your denials of error must be postulated on your clear declarations of Truth, and your consciousness of Truth must be so clear that your denials of error will not lead you into a material sense of thinking while you are making the denial.

As I have said so many times, there is no form which can be given for a treatment. The Truth heals, and your knowledge of Truth will heal without specific application. If, for instance, you were to sit down to do your daily work for yourself, you, of course, would be in a better position than anyone else to know what needed most to be handled in your consciousness. No one could tell you what to take up further than what anyone would take up and handle. In the first place, you would know what God is and what man is. That is, you would try and get a clear vision that all that has ever existed is one infinite Mind.

Creation must consist of something, and if creation is the outcome of some great first Cause, that great first Cause must be the only Cause, and consequently could not have created that which would have power or desire to disrupt the harmony of its own creation. Because the great first Cause could not have created a destructive force which it in itself did not contain, we must conclude that the creation of the great first Cause must be perfect, intact, eternal, and right here and now; and that consequently, there can be no lesser or disrupting creation; and that what seems to be a lesser or inharmonious creation is not a lesser creation; in fact, is no creation at all, but simply an illusion. If it is an illusion, what is it an illusion of? The answer is *mortal mind*. But there is no mortal mind because the great first Cause could not create or be reflected in anything inferior to Himself. Hence there is no counterfeit creation, and because there is no counterfeit creation, your declarations of Truth must be based on Truth alone without any relative sense, and without the possibility of a lesser creation out of which we must emerge before entering the spiritual and eternal. Therefore, the picture of a universe filled with spiritual ideas which were never born, and which involve no matter and no process of matter, and of which your patient is one, is the picture you must hold constantly in thought.

Your patient was never born; he never knew anything about matter or a material body; he was never under any influence but the divine Mind, Life, Truth and Love. From this basis you will see how difficult it would be for your patient to come under any laws of sickness or inharmony because Spirit, or its idea, can never be sick, can never have sensation, pain, or be conscious of inharmony. Treat your patient in thought just as you would consider God in thought. Your patient is a reflection of God no matter what he may think he is. Suppose, just for argument or clarification, you had before you in such a way that you could designate it or individualize it, a tangible right idea. Suppose you had before you the idea of Love. Now, that idea of Love could never be sick, could it? That idea of Love could never be embodied in matter, could it? It could not take the form of a mortal, could it? It could not be conscious of pain, of poverty, inharmony, and the like, could it? In fact it couldn't be conscious of anything but itself, could it?

Now, suppose you had over in another part of the room a material person, flesh embound, having a mind of his own, capable of experiencing pain and pleasure in matter, capable of being sick, inharmonious and poverty stricken, capable of being sinful and subject to the whims and influences of other minds, desires and suggestions. There you have two distinct and separate objects. One of them is not familiar with, does not know, and is not conscious of the other. One does not know the other exists. They never mingle, and never become conscious of each other. The idea of Love, the idea of divine Mind, has always existed. It was never born; it has never changed; it never dies; it will never be subject to any of the claims, laws or limitations of mortal mind because as far as it is concerned no such mind exists. The divine idea of Love is conscious only of the Mind which created it, and that is the only Mind there is; therefore, there is no other creation as far as that divine idea of Love is concerned. The mortal person which sits over in the other part of the room was born to sense, lives in matter, can be sick, poverty stricken, and the like, all of which is the manifestation of a mind which God never created.

Now, in your mental attitude in treating a patient, all that you have to consider — in fact, all that exists — is that divine idea of Love. The other does not exist, never has existed, and is just as far removed from the divine idea which your patient is in reality as the mortal personage which sat in the other part of the room was away from the divine idea of Love. The two never mingle. They never meet, and they are not to be confused or commingled in giving a treatment. The divine idea of Love which you have before you is all there is, and what you can declare about that divine idea of Love, you can declare about your patient, whether that patient is yourself or someone else.

Forget about the material man when you are giving a treatment. Forget about creation in a material sense. There never was a creation in the spiritual sense. Everything that exists now always has existed as a spontaneous expression or evidence of the all-inclusive and self-existent Mind or Consciousness. God is Consciousness, and man is the conscious expression of that Consciousness. Man can never be conscious of anything but God because there is nothing else in existence. There is not any error. The very term *error* excludes itself from the realm of the real because error is that which is not true, and, as that which is not true does not exist, there is no error. Error is the opposite of Truth, and man reflects Truth. Remember that man is expression and not suppression. I shall touch briefly on that a little later.

Giving a Daily Treatment

If, then, you were giving yourself a daily treatment how would you go about it? What would necessarily be your first step? The very first thing you would have to do, either in giving yourself a treatment or in giving a treatment to another, would be to get into consciousness a clear understanding of God. You would, in your thinking, declare that God is the divine Principle of the only universe there is. God is the Mind which initiates, promulgates and includes all existence; you would become clearly conscious that this Mind is infinite, fills all space, and is the only source of intelligence or being there is; that this Mind imparts only its own qualities, and that this Mind includes and encompasses all existence; that this Mind is expressed through ideas which possess and maintain all the qualities of their divine source; that all volition, action, being consciousness, lie within this Mind; that this Mind is all-inclusive, and contains and includes nothing outside itself.

You would know that God is Life, and that God is infinite, and that hence Life fills all space, and that in Life there can be no suggestion of mortality, disintegration, organization, matter, or sickness. Nothing can be included in Life that does not exist in divine Mind; that divine Mind and Life are one, and that both are eternal and infinite and omnipotent; therefore there are no lives many; Life is not divided into lives many; there is but one Life, and man is the expression of that one Life and has no life of his own to lose; therefore man's life is not subject to matter, disorganization, time, sickness or anything less than life. In Life there is no death and no death process because there are nothing but the ideas of Mind included in Life. Life never fades, grows dim, or is lost because Life is the same yesterday, today and forever. Life is God in action, and God is ever-active because He is ever-present.

You would know that God is the divine Principle of all the vast universe of ideas; that this divine Principle fills all space, and is the only Principle governing the universe of ideas because divine Principle expresses the intelligence and wisdom of Mind, and therefore includes in its operation, control and supervision only that which is included in the divine Mind; that everything in the universe of God, everything in the universe of divine ideas, is under the control, supervision, direction and protection of this one infinite divine Principle which regulates everything within the scope of Mind with unerring accuracy; that this Mind or Principle never forgets; that it is all inclusive, and that therefore the ideas of Mind cannot be forgotten, sequestered or ignored.

You would know that God is Truth, and that this Truth is infinite, filling all space, and that because of this infinity, there can be no error in all of this vast universe of ideas. Error is the supposititious absence of Truth, and as Truth is infinite and fills all space, there is no error; that this infinite Truth permeates and includes all existence, and therefore cannot be tainted by or conscious of error.

You would know that this great universe of ideas, being governed by this one infinite Mind and Principle, expresses the Soul of the divine; that the consciousness of this divine Mind, expressed, constitutes the Soul of the universe; that the Soul of the universe is God, and therefore the Soul of the universe is divine Consciousness; and that the universe in its entirety is conscious of nothing that does not come from Soul.

You would know that God, being infinite Mind and Principle and Soul, filling all space, not bounded by matter or material beliefs, must be Spirit, because nothing of a finite nature could be infinite and unconfined; that Spirit is constituted of this divine Mind; that it includes all Life; that it fills all space; that the universe of God's creating is the spontaneous reflection or expression of Spirit. If God were not Spirit, He would not and could not be infinite. Nothing but Spirit could be infinite.

You would also know this Mind which constitutes God is Love, and that the expression of Love is the universe; that because there is nothing in the universe but Love, there can be no hate, no curse, no malice, no diabolical mind and no mortal mind. On the basis of one creator and one creation, without even an opposite or contradicting creation, rests the potency and efficacy of your treatment.

Having built this firm foundation of a consciousness of God, you then proceed in your treatment to man, or the patient. To gain this clear concept of God and man as herein outlined, you will, of course, not require the time that it takes to outline the operation here. Convictions are spontaneous and instantaneous, and are arrived at momentarily whereas the explanation of this operation takes much more time than is necessary to use in giving a treatment. However, the more time you spend in the contemplation of God, and the clearer you become as to Him and His exclusive creation of man, the better will be your treatment. Your next step in order in your treatment is man.

Treating Man through the Synonyms

If God is Mind, man must be an idea of that Mind, because there is no other creator. Mind must be expressed in harmony, peace, understanding, knowledge and wisdom. Man is the spontaneous expression of that creative Principle which Mrs. Eddy has termed

Mind, and therefore man must be as perfect as the Mind which he expresses. Because there is but one Mind, man cannot express anything but this one Mind. There can be no argument or belief of confusion, misunderstanding, misdirection or indecision in man, for man expresses the all-knowing, all-seeing, all-wise Mind. No concept of matter or a material mind can ever enter the consciousness of man because there is no mortal mind. God never created a mind separate from Himself to disrupt or disorganize His own creation. Man is an idea of the one and only Mind there is, and therefore is held, supported, supplied, sustained and nourished by the Mind that created him. Man is obedient to God. He has no will, volition, discretion or purpose of his own. He is the involuntary expression of Mind, and can be governed by no other influence. The government of man is in Mind, and therefore man has no responsibility of his own.

Man as an idea of Mind, as a compound idea of Mind, expresses Life. There is but one Life, and man expresses that Life. There is one Life only. Man has no life of his own. He has no life to lose, and his life is not subject to matter, mortal mind or death, because none of these exist. Life is eternal, and man has always existed inseparable from Life, a complete expression of Life and an idea of Life. As God, Life, is eternal, man, an idea of Life and inseparable from Life, must be eternal and changeless. There is no death process in Life; there is no sickness nor disorganization in Life; hence there can be no death or disorganization in the idea which expresses Life. Life is not subject to birth, growth, maturity or decay. Life never was conceived; it never germinated. It has always existed and is eternal. Life expresses activity. Activity in Science is the ever-presence of right ideas. Therefore man expresses activity because man includes all right ideas. There is no inaction, over-action or retarded action. Mrs. Eddy tells us, "Growth is the eternal mandate of Mind." Therefore growth does not mean accretion, enlargement or accumulation. It means the eternal manifestation of that which has always existed. This is well to know in handling the belief of false growth, etc. Growth and development are not processes of matter cognizable by the physical senses. Growth and development are simply significant of the unfoldment of the truths of existence in consciousness, and therefore there is no underdevelopment, arrested growth, retarded growth, overgrowth, etc. There are a myriad of claims of mortal mind which may be included in Life as applied to God.

Man, as a compound idea of Mind, must be spiritual. There is nothing in Mind out of which matter could be created; therefore man, as spiritual, cannot be flesh embound. He was never born; he never passes through any experience of material conception or birth. He was never thrust out of his original state of existence in God and born into matter. The senses of man are all spiritual, and every sense of man is an idea in Mind. Man, as the image of God, partakes of the body of Christ, the members of which are fitly joined together under one infinite intelligence. The expression of spiritual ideas through man constitute man's embodiment, his consciousness, his environment, his being and his experience. Therefore man can be conscious of nothing but what God sends, and he can experience only that which God has ordained, and he expresses only that which comes from God. All the ideas of Mind which are expressed through man as faculties, functions, members, etc., are coordinated and synchronized under the control and operation of the one infinite intelligence, and therefore there is no inharmony, no conflict of ideas in man, no friction, no irritation, no inflammation. Harmony is the law of the one infinite intelligence which governs the ideas which constitute the universe including man. Man is the reflection and expression of all the ideas of Mind included in the universe, and because of this inclusion of ideas, man has dominion. Man has dominion through reflection, and therefore man is subject to nothing but God, and can be under no other influence or control but that of God, because there is no other influence or Mind but the divine.

Man, expressing the Mind of God, being the representation of God through ideas, reflects God as Soul. The consciousness of man is God, and God is Soul and Soul is divine Consciousness. Therefore the soul of man is the consciousness of man, and as there is but one Mind and that Mind is God, man's consciousness must be divine. As there is but one Mind, the soul of man cannot be tainted with or influenced by the belief of any lesser mind or creation. There are not minds many, gods many, wills many, nor purposes many; therefore there is no recreation, procreation, counterfeit or material creation, and consequently no belief of a counterfeit or material creation can ever enter divine Consciousness to defile or disorganize the creations of that consciousness, or man. Man remains intact, inviolate, pure, holy and spiritual throughout all time. He cannot be interfered with by birth, rebirth, sensuous existence, matter or mortal mind. There is no mortal mind; therefore there is no matter. There isn't even an illusion, because illusion presupposes a mind which is capable of becoming illusioned or disillusioned. Matter is not the outcome of mortal mind because there is in reality no mortal mind. Matter is simply the supposititious absence of spiritual existence; and as there is nothing in all creation but spiritual existence, there can be no matter, even in illusion. Like darkness, matter does not exist. It is simply the supposed absence of light. The moment light appears, there is no darkness. The darkness does not go anywhere to stay away in hiding while the light is around. It simply isn't. The same with illusion, matter, mortal mind. They don't exist in the light of divine understanding, and you therefore have not those to handle in your treatments. You simply affirm and realize the allness of God and His creation, and that in itself dispels the illusion, matter, mortal mind, animal magnetism, etc.

Expression versus Suppression

Man, remember, is expression. That will help you often in treatments. Man is expression. He is not suppression or depression. Man cannot withhold. He has to express and give. Giving is expressing, and expressing is man. Man has no other alternative, because giving, or expressing, is the nature of man as the image of God. Watch thought that it becomes expression, and not suppression or depression.

One time a lady came to me with a severe physical condition of which she wished to be healed. It was one which involved a growth, a bearing down, an inflamed, swollen and obstructing condition. She could walk but a short distance without pain and a sense of bearing down and pressure which was rapidly making it impossible for her to get about at all. On talking with her a few times, I discovered that her whole mental attitude was one of suppression. She was not expressing. She was suppressing human emotions, sentiments, etc. She was heavy in mind, timid, self-conscious, retiring, more or less liable to resentment and aloofness, self-pitying and extremely quiet and expressionless. There was no joy there. It developed that the same mental characteristics were a family trait. She was an abject object of suppression. She harbored carnal thoughts which, in itself, prevented her from expressing divine ideas. We took this up, worked on it and finally got a freer sense of expression. She let loose of some of her nurtured mortal mind convictions. She began to express joy and love and freedom. We handled heredity, the belief that she was ever born, that she lived in matter and that she had human parents who could dictate the nature of her existence through heredity, and she finally became free. She was simply an example of suppression and had no sense of expression, although she had been in Christian Science a long time.

✗ + + [Love is not Love until it is expressed. More freedom, more joy, more health, more harmony, more abundance can be demonstrated by simple and concrete expressions of love than all the love in the world seemingly held in consciousness and hoarded or withheld. When you express and send out love, you are then coming into your birthright as a son of God. Expression is man. That is what man is — the expression of God. If God, for instance, is Love and man is His image or expression, man cannot withhold love. He must express it. He cannot help but express it. He isn't man unless he is expressing love. Man is a transparency for Truth. He has no volition. He is not man unless he expresses. So, let us all begin right now to see if we cannot become more consciously children of God by expressing those qualities of Mind, which in reality are ours, and which in reality we do express, but are not conscious of.

A divine idea expressed in your consciousness constitutes your real manhood. The same idea, suppressed, or held in your thought as something nice, but which you refuse to express, is worth nothing in your experience. Freedom of expression around your home, among your friends and associates will help you more than anything else. As someone has said, a candle which you have placed in your own window to guide you home at night, not only helps you, but it is a beacon of cheer and comfort to everyone who comes your way.

Man as the expression of Truth, which fills all space and which admits and knows nothing unlike itself, cannot be conscious of error. Truth means simply the absence of error, and as man is the expression of Truth, he can be conscious of only that which is included in the divine Mind. In this all-knowing intelligence or Principle there is no error. You can always declare for your patient that which you declare about God. You may declare that your patient knows everything that God knows, and that he is conscious only of the things of God. In fact, you will have to declare for your patient that which would be true of him if there were no material world, no matter, no carnal mind, no error — because that is the truth about him, and the truth about him is what makes free. The only mind there is, is Love, and man as the expression of Love can never be conscious of hate, or anger, or any of the so-called qualities of the so-called mortal mind.

Handling Animal Magnetism in Treatment

Now, with this foundation laid of God, and man in God's image and likeness, you may proceed to take up all the various claims which the patient is trying to get rid of. Remember that error, sickness, poverty, old age, inharmony of any name or nature, come to you as a practitioner simply by way of suggestion trying to enter your consciousness, and that your work as a practitioner is to refuse this error admission into your consciousness. With the correct foundation in thought as to God and man, you affirm all the truth you know about man, and you deny all the error which is presented for admission to your consciousness.

In your daily work for yourself, with the foundation which you have laid through your contemplation of God and man, as above outlined, you may proceed to claim your own sonship with God, free from the arguments of animal magnetism expressing themselves in the form of human birth, growth, maturity, decay, old age, heredity, laws of astrology, planetary control, solar, lunar and stellar attraction, spiritualism, theosophy, mesmerism, hypnotism, curse, diabolism, sin, sickness, human or personal characteristics, greed, dishonesty, sensualism, Roman Catholicism, Judaism, occultism, false theology, ancient or modern necromancy, ancient or modern philosophy, electricity, the unity of error, esoteric magic, etc.

Now this is quite a long list of grievances, but they all have their supposed claims, and you will find them bobbing up at one time or another in the most unusual manner and under the strangest of circumstances. It is well to know that there is no unity of error or evil. Like God, good, error makes claim to a like unity. As there is and always has been a unity of good, which unity is never broken or interfered with by the claims of mortal mind, no evil can claim to present a united front or a unity which would offer an invincible front to the attacks of Truth.

There claims to be a mysterious and unexplainable sympathy between different and differing manifestations of the carnal mind — a unity, a sort of co-ordination or co-operation — a sympathetic bond. Take for example, the three different phases of mortal consciousness. First, the span of human life. Second, the world. Third, a day. These three phases of mortal existence all seem to include and express a striking similarity and sympathy which might suggest to one the deep and more hidden claims of mortal mind. Human life, for instance, has its period of conception, germination, birth, growth, maturity, decline, death.

The day of human experience has its birth at dawn. It proceeds on its course to its zenith of noon, its maturity; after which it begins to decline, and ends in the darkness or oblivion of night and is gone. The year has its germinating period in the cold and dark days of the winter season. It then blossoms forth into birth, or spring, and is born into all the glories of youth and hope. In the summer months it arrives at its zenith, or high noon of maturity. In the fall or autumn, after the period of fruition, it begins to decline and fade away — and then comes the death of all things which the youth of spring has brought forth, and again we find the winter upon us with the dead past a thing to be forgotten. In just these three manifestations of human existence, do you not perceive therein the claim of the unity of error or evil — the similarity, the coincidence, the sympathy between these different phases of mortal mind? And, may not this give us some glimpse of the deeper and hidden sources of the tenacity of error in many of its forms?

We should know daily that there is no unity of error, no sympathy of interest, effort, intent or purpose between elements or so-called manifestations of mortal mind. Error does not present a united front which is invincible and against which the shafts of Truth strike in vain. All of these claims of mortal mind — the material world, the solar year, the life of mortal man, and the course of a day — have no origin or existence in the great First Cause, and therefore do not exist as material phenomena. They exist as objectifications of a mind which does not exist. We might be inclined to give them some place or authority by saying they are manifestations of mortal mind, but when we ask ourselves the question as to who made mortal mind, we then have put these claims out of existence entirely — even as false claims.

One great fault in our thinking — in fact, I think the greatest fault — is that we make a claim of mortal mind, or a claim of error, just as real as the error itself would claim to be. That is, we merely substitute words for words. We don't substitute ideas for words as we should. We change words in our mental attitude. A claim of error is often — more than often — just as real to us in thought as error itself. We love to use the verbiage, or vernacular of Christian Science, but fail to change our thinking to accord with our use of terms. There is not much difference to the average Christian Scientist when you come right down to the facts in the case, between smallpox and the term a claim or belief of smallpox. There is not much difference in the thought of the average Christian Scientist between matter and a belief of matter. We make the belief of matter just as real as matter, and then wonder why we do not heal the sick. A belief of matter, for instance, is what? It is the manifestation of mortal mind and not the divine Mind. Where did mortal mind come from? Who made it and where is it? God certainly did not make it; and if God did not make it — and is the great First Cause and only Creator — then there never was, and is not, a mortal mind. If there is no mortal mind, there isn't any misconception of mortal mind or matter. So, do not work against something real, or something which is a mistaken concept of the true. There is no mistaken concept of the true to work against.

Right now you are a child of God, and you dwell in the divine consciousness as a perfect concept in Mind, free from matter or any of the manifestations of matter. You are not conscious of a material existence, or error, to be overcome, or of anything outside the divine consciousness. That is because the divine consciousness fills all space, and there is no counterfeit consciousness nor counterfeit creation. You have never ever been born. You have never been outside the divine consciousness. You never had a beginning. You never had a material father or mother. You never came under any law of material conception or birth. God is your Father and Mother. You have always existed as an eternal concomitant of divine Mind. You have never been outside the divine consciousness. Therefore there is no belief of a historical past, past conditions, past life, past history, past habits, past experiences or influences which can operate to fasten on you any belief of error. This is because error has no past, no present and no future, and man has never been anything less than man — the perfect, eternal image and likeness of God.

Man is an idea in Mind. He is a compound idea — expressing or reflecting all the ideas of Mind, and is, therefore, obedient only to the dictates and influences of that divine intelligence which governs and controls all His vast creation of ideas in perfect harmony and peace. The ideas of Mind, which each one of you here and now manifest, include your embodiment, your consciousness, your life, your being, and your experience. Therefore, you can be conscious, and are conscious, of nothing but God and His perfect creation — there is no lesser creation. Every one of your faculties is an idea which is governed, supported, sustained and supplied by the Mind which holds and beholds it. You partake of the body of Christ, the members of which are fitly joined together under one infinite intelligence. Therefore, your members, your faculties — all the ideas which are manifested through you — are coordinated and synchronized under one omnipotent and intelligent Mind, which is all-knowing, all-wise, all-seeing, all-loving and eternal.

There can be no inharmony because everything in God's kingdom (and there is no other) is governed in perfect harmony by the Mind which conceives and controls the universe. Therefore, there is no interference, no friction, no electricity, no injury, no inflammation. All is harmony and peace, and there is no mind to conceive of any inharmony or to be conscious of anything but God and His perfect manifestation. Do not worry about how you are going to tie up your treatments, or to fit them with the conditions to be healed. There is nothing to be healed, so you do not have to worry about how to make your statements of Truth do the work they are supposed to do. "Truth," Mr. Cook has said, "is its own impulsion." Therefore, as there is no material condition to which to fit a treatment, you do not have to worry about how it shall be done. You just know the Truth, and God will do the rest.

Relating Man to God in the Treatment

The first thing in your treatment is to get a clear understanding of what God is — His allness, His infinity, His omniscience, His omnipresence, His omnipotence. Then you can mentally declare and perceive man as the image and likeness of God. It is often asked what Mrs. Eddy means by the statement in *Science and Health* that man "is the compound idea of God . . . " This means, of course, that man reflects, includes and expresses all the ideas of Mind. Man, for instance, reflects Spirit — hence, man is spiritual. If man is the idea of God and if God is Spirit, an idea of Spirit could not be material — it must be spiritual, completely devoid of any sense of matter or the material. If God is Mind and man is the reflection of God, then man must express only that which is contained in divine Mind. The idea of Mind would be found in intelligence, wisdom, spiritual understanding, perspicacity, etc.

If God is Love, then man as the idea of Love could express only love, kindness, gentleness, true affection, tenderness, and the like. In other words, Love is expressed in loving — loving thoughts, loving deeds, etc. If God is Soul and man is the idea of Soul, man must reflect the consciousness of Soul. Soul is expressed in the term "divine consciousness." As man is the reflection of God, man must be the reflection of divine consciousness and of nothing else. Hence, divine consciousness is the Soul of man. If God is Life and man is the image of God, man must reflect Life. In the sense of God as infinite and eternal Life, there can enter no sense of mortality or death. Man is an idea of Life. Man has no life of his own. An idea cannot be separated from its origin, Mind, any more than a sunbeam can be separated from the sun. So man can never be separated from Life, nor can he be influenced by the thought of mortality or death. Man as an idea of Life has no life to lose. Life is one, infinite and eternal, and man is the idea of that one infinite and eternal Life.

If God is Truth and man is the image and likeness of God, man is an idea of Truth. If Truth fills all space and is everywhere present, then there is no error; and if there is no error, and man is the idea of Truth, man cannot be conscious of, nor can he express error, because there is none to express. There is no idea of error — and man is idea. Man as the compound idea of God signifies that man is the idea of all that is included in the synonyms — Mind, Spirit, Soul, Principle, Life, Truth, Love. Man, expressing all the ideas which could be conceived of as emanating from these synonyms, expresses these ideas in one consciousness. So, man is the compound idea of all the synonyms explaining God. Man includes all these ideas, and he includes nothing else. Thus we find that the foundation for all our treatments in Christian Science is the clear concept of God and man in His image and likeness. With this clear foundation firmly established in consciousness, you may proceed to the handling of any argument which presents itself, because every argument of mortality which might present itself to you for healing would be the opposite or contradiction of one of the synonyms of God — if not all of them.

The right understanding of God and man in His image and likeness, is a necessary prelude to the healing of sickness, poverty and the like. Every claim of mortal mind, so-called, will be met and mastered by the intelligent use of one or more of the synonyms used in Mrs. Eddy's definition of God. Now, by this, I do not mean that for every particular phase of mortal mind there is a particular synonym — or that for every synonym there is a particular and well-defined error. Nothing of that nature must enter into your concept of a treatment. But, as the synonyms which Mrs. Eddy has used in her definition of God include and express all of God, and as an understanding of God is necessary to the handling of error, it becomes clear that in some of the synonyms of God can always be found that idea which will meet and destroy the particular claim of error at hand.

The claim of death, of course, naturally finds its master in the understanding of God as Life. The thought of Life as God includes all that goes to make up life. If the claim is inaction, which is supposed to end in death, then the conquering idea is action, which constitutes an expression of life. Man includes action. Man, it may be said, expresses action — but, to be more specific, it can be said that man includes action. Action is an idea and not a material process. In handling cases which involve inaction, or over-action, or action in any of its phases, you will employ the synonym Life — knowing that in Life there is no inaction, reaction, etc., because there is but one Life; that man reflects this Life; that Life is not in man and therefore man has no life to lose. Man reflects Life, and because he reflects Life, he is man; he could not be man if he did not reflect Life. He could not help but express Life because he is an expression of Life. If Life had no expression, there would be no man; and if there were no man, there would be no Life. Life and man are inseparable. One cannot exist without the other.

The same may be said of Mind and Truth and Spirit. For instance, in the use of the term *Spirit* as a synonym of God, some time ago a lady came to me in a very serious physical condition. She was in such severe condition that I went to her — to be exact. She could not walk, or lie down, or stand up. All she could do was to sit up in a chair filled with pillows. After several talks with her, it developed that some time previously she had gone to another state to attend the funeral of her mother whom she loved dearly, and who was very much attached to her. Immediately after the funeral this particular trouble began to manifest itself. The thought immediately came to me of "spiritualism" — that man, after death, has the power of communication with those who have been left behind; that there is often a longing and a beckoning, and a desire to be reunited, either on the part of the deceased or those left behind; and that there is a sense that the dead have gone away somewhere, that there is a separation, a gulf which can be bridged through the belief of communications between the departed and those present. While I could see that the patient herself had no desire to go on to meet her mother, or that she herself had no idea or sense of spiritualism, it came to me very clearly that that was the very thing which was trying to manifest itself. I started to work on that one particular phase of error. Immediately improvement began, and there was a most marked and rapid change for the better.

I never mentioned the topic of spiritualism to the patient, as I could see she was not consciously any party to the belief. Nevertheless that seemed to be the very thing that was back of the condition, and it yielded most beautifully to the treatment. I knew that God was Spirit, and that there is but one plane of existence, and that man never passed off of that plane of existence to another plane of existence. I knew that there was no material plane of existence on which man lived, and that there was no unknown nor mysterious plane of existence to which he passes after death. I knew that there is but one Spirit, God — and that man is the image and likeness of that one Spirit. Therefore, man is not Spirit, he is spiritual, and there are not spirits many. As there is no passing from one plane to another, there is no separation, and consequently no longing or grief or sorrow at the loss of a departed one — because there is no departed one. Everything God ever created is here and now, completed and complete. There is no re-creation process, there is no rebirth, there is no material growth, development or maturity. Everything is here and now complete and always has been complete. There is no change called death that can interfere with God's creation. Man's position in that creation is as a child of God. I handled the whole situation from the standpoint of Spirit.

One could not undertake here to go through the vast array of mortal mind pictures to illustrate just how the use of the various synonyms of God may be applied, but you will find in your work that there will never be one case of error which you will not handle with one or more of the synonyms. Thus do we glimpse the importance of Mrs. Eddy's definition of God.

Astrology

Among the many phases of error which I mentioned in the list which I gave some pages back, I included the arguments or belief of astrology or planetary control I want to impress upon you the importance of handling that phase of animal magnetism. By way of explanation, some time ago a case of an underdeveloped child came to me. It was a belief of arrested development. It was a child, or boy, eighteen or twenty years of age with a mentality of a small child, and a most distorted and uncontrolled and uncontrollable physicality. At intervals that child would develop most aggravated expressions of spasms or convulsions. It was easy for me to see that the child's body had nothing to do with these spasmodic attacks. The body could not say to itself, now I guess I'll throw a fit or two and see how the boy likes that. The body had nothing whatever to do with it. The body was simply an illusion of the carnal mind, and therefore did not exist as matter or matter's expression. In fact, I could see clearly that the child did not live in the so-called material body — but that did not seem to be enough to stop these periodical spasmodic attacks.

The child lived at quite a distance, and I did not have much chance to talk with the parents. The child was in the care of a trained nurse most of the time — a Christian Science nurse. One day in talking with her over the phone about the conditions, she told me that she noticed that these attacks were more severe when the moon was at a certain quarter. I immediately took up work along that line, and those attacks became less and less from that very moment.

There is a very strong law of belief that all creatures are under the control of certain influences resulting from the condition of the sun, the moon, the planets, the stars, etc. The location and situation of the planets at the time of human birth are supposed to have some kind of influence over mortals. In the first place, one must know that man never was born. It must be understood that the patient never was in any place or position that God did not put him; that he never passed through any experience or condition that God did not create. Therefore, there is no belief of a historical past, past experiences, accidents, injuries, sad history, or influences that can operate to fasten on him any belief of error; that error, as Mrs. Eddy tells us, has no remote, predisposing or exciting cause; that the patient has never been born; that he has never been outside the divine Consciousness. God's concept of him has never changed, and God's concept of him is the only fact about him. Therefore, he has never been under any influence but the divine. Error cannot harm. Truth is the reality, and there is no unreality. Error has no object, no subject, no law of expression, no order, type, form or medium of expression. Man was never thrust out of Spirit and born into matter. He never passed through any experience of material conception, germination, development or birth. He does not live in matter, and is not subject to any of the so-called laws of matter or mortal mind claiming to fasten on him the arguments of family or ancestral traits, characteristics and inclinations — either of mind or body — because God is the Father and Mother of man, and man's inheritance is spiritual. Man is not an object of sense or sensuality, but is a pure, spiritual, holy concept of God.

In the case of this boy, by knowing that there is no electro-magnetic currents passing from the planets to man and controlling him; by knowing there is no matter, therefore matter cannot think, act, create, transmit or receive; by knowing that the pure strong currents of true spirituality constantly flow from God to man, furnishing him with life, vigor, strength and sustenance, the argument of spasmodic or uncontrolled action was met. Action is the ever-presence of all right ideas. As all right ideas are ever-present, there is therefore perfect action. There is no involuntary action. Matter has no intelligence of its own. There is no mortal mind to give it intelligence; therefore, there is no uncontrolled action. All action is under the control and direction of the divine will. Action is not a material process. Never try to bring about a right physical manifestation by visioning a material process. Right idea is action. Right ideas are everywhere, and they are everywhere without the material process of motion or movement.

Kindness is a right idea. Kindness, then, is action. The expression of love, honesty, peace and purity constitute divine action. Hence a patient, as a child of God, includes action. There is right action ever-present. We must watch lest we become confused in our treatments by the use of material terms. One has to use many times the term *action*, but we must watch lest the sense of material process gets into thought. For instance, in *Science and Health* Mrs. Eddy tells us that "... growth is the eternal mandate of Mind."

Our material concept of growth is one of material process, one of accretion, whereas all of God's creation exists here and now in its completeness, and nothing is ever changed, nothing added to or taken from it. "Christian Science presents unfoldment, not accretion; it manifests no material growth from molecule to mind, but an impartation of the divine Mind to man and the universe," we read in the textbook.

Growth then, as a "mandate of Mind," is one of unfoldment of ideas in consciousness. Ideas exist here and now in their completeness. In handling cases of arrested growth, such as the condition which mortal mind presents as an after-effect of infantile paralysis, one must know that creation or formation is a spiritual edict and not a material process. Therefore nothing in God's kingdom is arrested in its development. Everything exists here and now in its completeness. There is no underdevelopment or retarded, arrested, or deformed growth or development. A "mandate of Mind" is an idea of Mind which has existed eternally and is not the promulgation of a temporal command. A "mandate of Mind" is that which has existed from all eternity.

Electricity

Touching on the question of electricity, it might be well to quote from an article in which Dr. George W. Crilo of Cleveland gave his views. We find the medical profession (and I presume the same could be said of the physical scientists to a degree), advancing the following conclusions regarding electricity and the human body:

> Man is a mechanism run by electricity and chemical reaction — a machine made up of twenty-eight trillion electric cells. Every one of these twenty-eight trillion cells is a tiny wet battery with negative and positive poles. The brain cells are the most positive

> and the liver cells are the most negative. The greater the difference in electrical potential — the difference between positive and negative — the greater the energy. Fatigue or stress of emotions cuts down this difference; rest and sleep restore it. Electricity keeps the flame of life burning in the cell, and the cell — oxidation — supplies the electricity used in operating the animal. Emotions — love, hate, fear, jealously — are but stimulating processes, loosing currents of electricity through certain paths. Now, this, in simple terms, means that emotions let loose are like super-charges of electricity — they use up the previous energy of man. They destroy and in the end they can kill. Now, the two great electric magnets shooting off power are the glands near the brain and those next to the kidneys. The brain is the positive pole and the liver the negative pole. Adrenaline, excreted by the suprarenal bodies next to the kidneys, fires or vitiates a person's energies during the flares of hate, jealousy, fear, anger, according to the condition of the organs.

From this it can plainly be seen that electricity plays an important part in the work of a Christian Science practitioner. It will often be found necessary to consider this phase of error, whereas ignorance of the claim might leave one working more or less in the dark — in a rather round-about or circuitous course. We have all known that hate, malice, jealousy, fear, and worry have produced ill effects. When we are confronted with a case of sickness or material inharmony, either in ourselves or in others, we look for the hidden or controlling error in the case. Matter in itself has no authority, no mind, no intelligence, through which to express itself — either as sick or well, harmonious or inharmonious. Mortal mind is the author and the expression of human discord.

We have been successful in healing cases of illness or inharmony when we have been able to discover the mental cause of the so-called disease. If we have been confronted with a man with a bad disposition and a case of stomach trouble, we have been able to heal him of the stomach trouble by healing him of his bad disposition. We did not know exactly how the bad disposition — from the standpoint of physics or material reasoning — could affect the stomach. Nevertheless, we did know that by healing the disposition, we could heal the stomach.

Now comes along the explanation of how mortal mind accounts for all this disturbance. We find back of all this claim to physical inharmony, there lies the claim of electricity. Through the medium of so-called electrical forces set in motion or operation by the emotions — love, fear, hate, jealousy and the like — we find that the injurious effects of these emotions on man's so-called organs are accomplished. So may not many of the arguments with which we have been confronted and which perhaps we have been unable to readily heal, find their solution in our understanding of the nothingness of this claim of electricity? Take, for instance, cases of cancer with which material medicine has been so unsuccessfully coping for many years. According to the findings of material science, or material medicine, the only explanation of the claim of cancer lies in the so-called cell theory. It is claimed by medical authorities that the condition of cancer is a state of rebellion or riot among certain cells or group of cells of man's body.

A "cell riot" is the term used by *materia medica* to explain what it believes cancer to be. Now, with the added theory of cells of the human body as constituting myriads of little wet electrical batteries, all under the influence of electricity which is generated by our emotions, may we not confidently replace the argument of negative or destructive electrification of man by the positive of Spirit and know that man, existing in the image and likeness of God, is ever in his eternal state of spiritual wholeness and perfection, and that he can never be influenced or controlled by the claim of electricity superimposed through emotions which God did not create and with which, therefore, he is not familiar? There is no surplus of mortal mind out of which electricity could be produced. Therefore, there is no electricity that can influence or control the body of man.

Man partakes of the body of the Christ, the members of which are ideas of Mind which are fitly joined together under the regimentation and control of one infinite, loving and omnipotent intelligence. Every member of man, every faculty, is an idea of Mind, and these ideas are all coordinated and synchronized under one infinite and all-knowing intelligence. Man is not sequestered or forgotten. He is the eternal expression of an all-knowing Mind which fills all space, and never for an instant loses sight of every least idea of His vast system of ideas. There is no electrical force to cause a cell riot in man — man is not made up of cells. He is constituted of ideas. Cell riot is a form of rebellion. There is no rebellious thought, no resentment, repulsion or hatred in Mind.

I was very much interested in something which was told to me recently. A man who was suffering from cancer went to the Mayo Brothers. While there, he asked them what was the cause of the cancer. They told him that it was rebellion of some sort — that some particle in the physical body rebelled against normal function and added to itself through rebellion. This man was finally given up by them all. He went to Christian Science and was healed in Science. He saw that his own case was that of rebellion against certain conditions. To me, this was a most interesting uncovering of the causes of that belief.

There is nothing for man to rebel against. There is nothing with which he can rebel. Everything in his being is in accord with God and is manifesting God's love, plan, and purpose. There is no resistance to this plan and purpose, nor to taking up the cross and denying the beliefs of incurability calling themselves fears, sorrows, hatred, or difficult situations. Until we do take up the cross, we cannot follow where this Christ-Truth leads us — namely, to eternal harmony and our at-one-ment with our divine Principle, Love.

Mesmerism and Hypnotism Defined

I have on my desk a letter from a student which reads as follows: "My one big question is about animal magnetism, mesmerism and mental malpractice. What are they? How do they work? How do you recognize them in your experience? How do you protect yourself from them?" That one question, of itself, would furnish enough material for two or three association addresses if properly handled. In fact, it would involve, in a way, the entire twelve lessons of class instruction. Everything that has been said here has to do with the handling of animal magnetism. In the first place, it may be said that what we as Christian Scientists are seeking is not as much a knowledge of what animal magnetism is, as to what it is not. All error of every name or nature is animal magnetism. The belief of life, truth, intelligence in matter is animal magnetism. Magnetism is defined in the dictionaries as: 1) property, quality or state, of being magnetic; manifestation of that force in nature which is seen in a magnet. 2) the science of magnetic phenomena. 3) power to attract; power to excite the feelings and gain the affection. 4) hypnotism.

Now, we are not going to delve into the depths of animal magnetism today. We have not the time. But it may be said that the term *animal magnetism* as used by Mrs. Eddy is best described in its own terms. It is *animal attraction*, or the influence of animality. Animal magnetism may be said to be the supposititious influence of anything unlike God, good. The belief of intelligent matter, sensation in matter, pain or pleasure in matter, material existence, material birth, death, sickness, lack — all of the claims of mortal existence — are the claims of animal magnetism.

In the textbook Mrs. Eddy says, "As named in Christian Science, animal magnetism or hypnotism is the specific term for error, or mortal mind." Now, this is briefly and succinctly an explanation of animal magnetism. Any phase of material existence is the product of animal magnetism. In this definition of animal magnetism as quoted above, Mrs. Eddy also calls animal magnetism *hypnotism*. Material existence is a state of hypnotism or mesmerism. Hypnotism may be said to be the so-called influence or operation of one mortal mind over another, while mesmerism is self-inflicted. Hypnotism includes mesmerism, while mesmerism may not include hypnotism.

You and I admit into our consciousness so-called carnal thoughts which come to us from a supposititious mind which exists outside ourselves. These thoughts which you and I admit into our consciousness are objectified as matter, sin, sickness, etc. The matter — the sin and the sickness which you and I experience in our so-called material existence, or with which we come in contact — is self-created. This self-created material existence is a stage of mesmerism which may also be called hypnotism. We are self-mesmerized into believing in a material existence. This self-mesmerism might be said to be also a state of self-hypnotism. Matter does not exist. You and I, in our concepts of materiality are just self-mesmerized — like the man in the insane ward who thinks he is George Washington.

If one person were to willfully take possession of the mentality of another through the influence of manipulated and directed thought, and direct the thinking of that person — that would be hypnotism in its primitive state and would not involve mesmerism. Mesmerism may be said more specifically to be self-inflicted, whereas hypnotism may be said to be the willful control of one mortal mind over another mortal mind. Mental malpractice includes all wrong thinking, and may be detected readily by anyone who understands the teachings of Christian Science. All wrong thinking is mental malpractice, and there is no one on the face of this earth who is not in some degree a mental malpractitioner. As soon as you and I cease to be mental malpractitioners, we will cease to exist in the flesh.

It is a form of mental malpractice to believe that we live in a material body. We say we do not believe that we live in matter, but if we knew that we did not, we would not be conscious of a material body. As long as we are conscious of a material body, we are malpractitioners. There is a distinction, of course, between mental malpractice and malicious mental malpractice. Malicious mental malpractice is the use of thought intentionally directed to do personal harm or injury. Hate, malice, revenge and the like would come under malicious mental malpractice.

No one who is at all familiar with Christian Science and employs it in his daily thinking and living, could be long in doubt as to what mental malpractice is, or what malicious mental malpractice is. We have no time now to go into these phases of Christian Science; consequently, these topics in their general aspect can only be touched on briefly. The remedy for animal magnetism is Christian Science. Every right thought you entertain is handling a certain degree of animal magnetism. If you are in a quandary as to what animal magnetism is, consult the five physical senses. They will furnish you with a complete answer to the question of what animal magnetism is. It is also your answer to what mesmerism or hypnotism is, because the material state is not a state of matter — it is a state of mesmerism or hypnotism. Every thought which does not square with the teachings of Christian Science is mental malpractice. No one who knows how to think in Christian Science should not be in doubt as to what mental malpractice is, nor should he be in doubt as to how to detect it. Anyone who knows that twice five is ten is not long in doubt as to handle twice five is eleven. You protect yourself from twice five is eleven by your understanding that twice five is ten.

You protect yourself from hate by loving. You protect yourself from poverty and lack by giving. You protect yourself from the belief of man as indwelling matter or a limited body by understanding that man is expression, and not suppression or depression. You protect yourself from the belief that there is life, truth and intelligence in matter by the understanding that "All is infinite Mind and its infinite manifestation, for God is All-in-all." (*Science and Health*) You protect yourself from the shafts of malicious malpractice by love, by kindness, and by seeing your brother man as a child of God, incapable of hating or doing harm.

You never work against a malicious mental malpractitioner. You love him. You can't love him if you fear him or hate him. To fear him is to make that real which you would try to see as unreal. The only place an enemy or a hater can exist is in your own consciousness. You never would be conscious of, or become the victim of hate or malice or malicious mental malpractice, if the possibility of such a thing did not exist in your own consciousness — that is, unless error existed in your own thought. Don't ever worry about a malpractitioner or a hater. Be concerned as to your own thinking and correct that, and you will never suffer from another's wrong thought — no matter how evil or hateful those thoughts may claim to be.

As we close this meeting, I want to express my deep appreciation for your attendance here. The little part I play in meetings like this represents but a small fraction of what I get out of them myself. Really, getting comes from giving, and I find the more we give of time, of money, of effort, of thought, and the like, to our work in Christian Science, the more abundantly does the good God shower us with His blessings. Mental or spiritual contentment is the one big object in human endeavor. If we are bringing out a more abundant life in the joy and gladness we shower about us — in our home, in our work, in the shop — the greater will be our blessings from above.

Our work in Christian Science will be more greatly blessed as we drop the material as our objective and let our gaze rest solely on the spiritual. The spiritual is that which brings harmony into our endeavors. The less we hold the material in thought, the greater will become our harmony. Harmony is just one evidence of spirituality of thought, and the less concern we give to material objects and ends, and the more time we devote to spiritual pursuits, the happier we will be, the more abundant will be our life, and the easier our supply will come.

May this year be filled with the most joyful and soul-satisfying experiences of your life. Even though the way may seem at times beset by seeming odds, and the dark spectre of mortal sense may seem to hover close at hand, always remember that he who stands firmly against the evil one with the sword of Truth in his hand and the armour of Spirit girt about him, will emerge triumphantly from the clouds of sense into the glorious sunlight of his Father-Mother God.

Holy Father, Thou hast taught us
We should live to Thee alone;
Year by year, Thy hand hath brought us
On through dangers oft unknown.

When we wandered, Thou hast found us;
When we doubted, sent us light;
Still Thine arm has been around us,
All our paths are in Thy sight.

We would trust in Thy protection,
Wholly rest upon Thine arm,
Follow wholly Thy directing,
Thou our only guard from harm.

Keep us from our own undoing,
Help us to turn to Thee when tried,
Still our strength in Thee renewing,
Keep us ever at Thy side.

ABOUT THE AUTHOR: William Duncan Kilpatrick was a native of Owosso, Michigan. He graduated from Olivet College in 1895, and from the University of Michigan with the degree of LL.B. in 1898. He practiced law for two years in Owosso, and from 1900 to 1907 in Washington, D.C., after which he was in the land and lumber business for several years.

Mr. Kilpatrick became interested in Christian Science in 1899, and became a member of The Mother Church in 1905. The same year he had primary class instruction. Several years later he left the business world, and entered the public practice of Christian Science in 1912.

For three consecutive years he was appointed Committee on Publication for Michigan. He left this work in 1917 upon election to membership on the Christian Science Board of Lectureship. Except for periods taken for the study of Christian Science, he lectured continuously in the United States and abroad until July of 1944. He became a teacher in 1919, holding his class and Association each year in Detroit.

He was made head of Committees on Publication at The Mother Church, The First Church of Christ, Scientist, in Boston, Massachusetts in July, 1944, and was serving in that capacity when he passed on.